MAKE IT REAL

IFRS ACCOUNTING AND FINANCE FOR REAL ESTATE

SECOND EDITION

By

Etim O. Uso

Gloria O. Ejekukor

MAKE IT REAL

IFRS ACCOUNTING AND FINANCE FOR REAL ESTATE

CONTENTS

PREFACE

The Real Estate industry has remained one of the most vibrant all over the world and it will remain so for as long as human beings keep multiplying on earth. Despite a few occasional hiccups, this industry has a way of adjusting itself and bouncing back with renewed vigour.

There are various levels of players and actors in the real estate sector. While some have professional training and high-level education, the majority do not. However, based on our experience working in this sector, we have found out that one area that has not received the rigorous treatment it deserves, even among real estate professionals, is accounting. In this era of big data and universal visibility, there is an urgent need to harness all the resources at our disposal to create a smart and robust environment for more efficient management and excellent service delivery in the sector. Such a system must, among other things, incorporate Standards and requirements, prescribed for global best practices, especially in areas of financial management and reporting.

Real Estate accounting demands holistic compliance with all the relevant provisions of the **International Financial Reporting Standards (IFRS)**. The core Standards applicable to the Real Estate include:

- **IAS 40**—Investment Property
- **IAS 16**—Property, Plant and Equipment
- **IAS 2**—Inventory
- **IFRS 16**—Leases (formerly IAS 17)
- **IFRS 15**—Revenue from Contracts with Customers (which merges what was formerly Revenue (IAS 18) with The Construction Contract (IAS 11) and all the previous Interpretations (IFRICs) on Revenue

Some of the parameters that determine the appropriate Standards and policies to apply in any given situation are:

a) Ownership of the property, and whether it is an investment property of owner-occupied.
b) Whether the property is meant for sale or lease.
c) Whether the property is meant for Operating or Finance Lease.

Apart from accounting for Investment Properties meant for sale or lease, Real Estate entities that are also engaged in the construction of Real Estate projects must comply with IFRS 15 in accounting for these projects—from Work-in-Progress to completion.

Real Estate accounting is so onerous that only a handful of companies can meet the disclosure requirements of the IFRS. This book is an effort to collate all the Standards and Interpretations that apply to real estate entities in one volume and present them in a coherent way that aligns with the operational workflow of real estate transactions.

The book is a response to our observations while implementing custom information management solutions for real estate companies over the past ten years. We have noticed the absence of a comprehensive guide or manual that provides holistic treatment for real estate accounting and bookkeeping. This book is meant to fill that gap. We have not invented any new rule or method. All we have done is to provide a clear, simple, and practical guide on how to account for real estate transactions in accordance with the provisions of the International Financial Reporting Standards (IFRS).

MAKE IT REAL is, therefore, a book on Real Estate accounting—a manual for keeping the books of real estate entities—in accordance with the classification, measurement, recognition, and presentation policies of the **International Financial Reporting Standards** (IFRS).

This book is not about the administrative and legal issues involved in Real Estate accounting and finance. Our goal is to provide computational guidance that can lead to the design and implementation of effective and reliable financial information management systems for the Real Estate sector. Some of the calculations in this book were tested using **ExpressBook iPMA** investment property management and accounting software.

The first edition of this book had an introductory chapter on the fundamentals of accounting and bookkeeping. That chapter is no longer available in this edition, as there are volumes of materials elsewhere that can provide such basic knowledge. We have intentionally decided to focus on only those IFRSs that are relevant and mandatory to Real Estate. These Standards include:

1) Revenue
2) Construction Contract (and its application to the Construction of Real Estate Property)
3) Leases
4) Investment Property
5) Property Plant and Equipment
6) Inventory

Although Construction Contract and Revenue (and all other Revenue-related Interpretations) have been collapsed into one Standard, we have chosen to treat the two separately for clarity. Moreover, we still prefer to refer to those interceptions, which are now merged with Revenue (IFRS 15) with their former names. These include IFISC 12 and 15.

The last chapter of this book focuses on financial calculations relevant to real estate—something many people find intimidating. We have simplified these calculations by providing detail explanations and solved examples to aid practical understanding for both professional and non-professionals. The list of calculations included in this book is as follows:

a) Future Value (FV)
b) Sinking Fund Factor (SFF) and Sinking Fund Schedule
c) Present Value (PV)
d) Annuity
e) Discounted Cash Flow (DCF)
f) Internal Rate of Returns (IRR)

We hope this book will add tremendous value to your skill and expertise as a player in the real estate sector. Combined with our real estate accounting and financial software solution, **ExpressBook iPMA**, there is no doubt you will have a unique experience that will take the burden off your back and free you to focus on making decisions that matter most.

Etim O. Uso
Gloria O. Ejekukor

CHAPTER 1

REVENUE RECOGNITION

Revenue remains the most important item in the chart of accounts of all profit-oriented entities—irrespective of size, industry, or geographic location. A company is identified by its revenue streams more than anything else. In this chapter, we will be looking at IFRS accounting policies (the measurements, recognition, and classification policies) for revenue. But before we do that, it is necessary to understand the difference between Revenue and Income, to keep abreast with the disclosure requirements of IFRS.

THE DIFFERENCE BETWEEN REVENUE AND INCOME

In some contexts and ordinary conversations, the terms *revenue* and *income* are used interchangeably. However, their formal accounting definitions connote something different. **Income** is defined as an "increase in economic benefits in the form of inflows or enhancements of assets or decreases in liabilities that result in increases in equity, other than contributions from equity holders" during a specified period. **Revenue**, on the other hand, is that part of income that is attributed to the **ordinary activities of an entity** (and excludes **gains** such as profit on the disposals of noncurrent assets, foreign exchange translation, fair value adjustments, etc.). Thus, **income is equal to revenue plus gains**. In this book, I may be using the two terms—revenue and income—interchangeably, but in your chart of accounts, make sure you separate **revenue** from **other income** and disclose them separately in your Income Statement.

In this book, we use the term "Rental Income" for convenience and ease of understanding. Rental Income is revenue to real estate entities and should be classified as such. However, that will not be the case for a financial service or an oil and gas entity that earns rent from its leased assets.

RECOGNITION OF REVENUE

Formerly, **IAS 18**, Revenue has now been combined with all other Revenue-related Standards and Interpretations (such as the IAS 11, IFRIC 12 and 15) to become **IFRS 15**. This is the Standard that prescribes the criteria for the classification, measurement, recognition, and presentation of revenue. The key issue with income or revenue recognition is timing—at what point in a transaction should an entity recognize revenue?

The revenue recognition framework under IFRS 15 is quite complicated. In this chapter, we will only deal with the essential elements of revenue recognition in IAS 18, which have been carried over to IFRS 15.

Essentially, revenue recognition under IAS 18 deals with the following types of revenue: **sales of goods**; **provision of services**; **royalties, and dividends**. It excluded income from other sources covered by different standards, such as Leases (IFRS 16); dividends from equity method of investments (IAS 28); Insurance Contracts (IFRS 4); Changes in Fair Values of Financial Instruments (IAS 39), and current assets; Initial Recognition and Change in Fair Values of Biological Assets (IAS 41) and Initial Recognition of Agricultural Produce (IAS 41).

RECOGNITION OF REVENUE—SALE OF GOODS

Revenue from the **sales of goods** can only be recognized when the following conditions are met:

a) The entity has transferred to the buyer the significant risks and rewards of ownership of goods.
b) The entity retains neither continuing managerial involvement to the degree usually associated with ownership nor effective control over the goods sold.
c) The amount of revenue can be measured reliably.
d) It is probable that the economic benefits associated with the transaction will flow to the entity; and
e) The costs incurred or to be incurred in respect of the transaction can be measured reliably.

However, what constitutes "significant risks" is left to judgment.

Expenses associated with revenue (such as cost of goods, along with all associated overhead costs) should be recognized simultaneously with revenue within the same transaction.

These provisions are quite clear and straight forward. Going by these provisions, you cannot recognize revenue:

a) when the goods sold are still in the seller's warehouse or are to be delivered to the buyer on a future date, even if the buyer has paid for the goods
b) if the buyer has not yet taken possession of the goods, and (in the case of property) if the legal title of ownership of the property has not been

transferred to the buyer, except properties acquired through a finance lease.

RENDERING OF SERVICES

When it comes to rendering services, the following recognition criteria apply:

a) The amount of revenue can be measured reliably.
b) It is probable that the economic benefits associated with the transaction will flow to the entity.
c) The stage of completion of the transaction at the balance sheet date can be measured reliably, and
d) The costs incurred for the transaction and the costs to complete the transaction can be measured reliably".

While the determination of **cost of sales** (for sales of goods) may be a straightforward affair, the determination of costs incurred for the provision of services may require more effort in the tracking of both the direct and overhead costs associated with the services.

Recognition of revenue for the rendering of services may require the use of the percentage completion method, whereby revenue is recognized based on the percentage of services already rendered. However, the probability of "economic benefits associated with the transaction" flowing to the entity will be higher if the percentage completion recognition criteria are written into the service contract.

In the case of service contracts where an entity receives advance payment to cover a specified number of months for which the expected service is meant to cover, such receipt should first be recognized as Unearned Revenue (a liability). The straight-line method can then be used to recognize revenue arising from the transaction every month.

INTERESTS, ROYALTIES, AND DIVIDENDS

The requirements for the recognition of interests, royalties, and dividends are as follows:

a) Interest shall be recognized using the effective interest method.
b) Royalties shall be recognized on an accrual basis in accordance with the relevant agreement.
c) Dividends shall be recognized when the shareholders' right to receive payment is established.

TIMING FOR RECOGNITION OF REVENUE & EXPENSE

Timing is especially important in the recognition of revenue and expense. Revenues that are not yet due for recognition (such as goods or services paid for but not yet delivered) should be classified as **Unearned Revenue (or Income)**, while payment made in advance for goods and services that have not yet been received should be classified as **Prepaid Expense**.

EARNED REVENUE

This is the income that has met all the criteria for recognition—sales of goods and services for which you have fulfilled all relevant contractual and legal obligations of transferring all the risks of ownership to the buyer. The accounting entries are as follows:

- □ Dr. Cash (or Customer)
- □ Cr. Revenue (Sales)

UNEARNED (OR DEFERRED) REVENUE

Here, we are dealing with transactions that have not yet met the criteria for recognition. For example, you have received payment for goods or services that you have not yet delivered or rendered. The following accounting entries apply to such transactions:

- □ Dr. Cash
- □ Cr. Unearned Revenue (Liability)

Note that Unearned Income is a liability account because what you have there is not yours yet until you fulfill all the necessary contractual or legal obligations. Note also that payment for the goods or services may not necessarily coincide with revenue recognition.

Recognition of Unearned Revenue

When the conditions for the recognition of revenue are met, you will have to make the following accounting entries to derecognize the liability (Unearned Revenue) and recognize your earned income:

- □ Dr. Unearned Income
- □ Cr. Revenue (Sales)

That will convert Unearned Income to Income.

EXPENSE INCURRED

These are expenses that have met all the criteria for recognition—you have received the goods or services with full benefits and risks of ownership. The following accounting entries apply:

- ☐ Dr. Expense
- ☐ Cr. Cash (or Supplier)

PREPAID EXPENSE

This is a situation where you have paid for goods or services, but you are yet to enjoy the full benefits of the goods or services you paid for. Examples include rents and subscriptions payable in advance. The following accounting entries apply:

- ☐ Dr. Prepaid Expense (Asset)
- ☐ Cr. Cash

Recognition of Prepaid Expense

When the conditions for recognition of expense are fully met, you can make the following accounting entries to recognize the expense:

- ☐ Dr. Expense
- ☐ Cr. Prepaid (or Accrued) Expense

Note that in the case of rents, you will have to recognize the expense based on equal monthly instalments until the entire amount is exhausted over the period. But in the case of goods or services, you may have to use percentage delivery or completion as a basis for the recognition of expense.

CHAPTER 2

ACCOUNTING FOR LEASES

If you are in the Real Estate business, there are certain challenges you cannot avoid or brush aside, no matter how much you try. However, the way many people respond to these challenges can make a huge difference between long-term success and failure. In the absence of lucid and clear guidelines or instructions, coupled with the dearth of reliable and effective tools, many have resorted to tackling things heuristically. Accounting for leases is one area many have concocted their methods and rules, which may not align with the requirements of the **International Financial Reporting Standards (IFRS)**.

In this section, our goal is to provide you with the simplest and clearest methods for dealing with the fundamental issues involved in lease accounting.

WHAT IS A LEASE?

IFRS 16 (which has now replaced IAS 17) defines a lease as *an agreement whereby the lessor conveys to the lessee in return for a payment or series of payments for the right to use an asset for an agreed period.*

Take note of the following:

    a) There is an *agreement*, and the *amount* involved is specified.
    b) The *duration* is specified.
    c) There is a *Lessor*—the person or entity that owns the leased asset.
    d) There is a *Lessee*—the person or entity that receive or uses the asset.

This definition will provide the basis for deciding whether a transaction can be regarded as a lease—and not the legal contents of the agreement (*substance over form*).

Inception of a Lease

This is the date of lease agreement or the date the parties involved in the lease agreement commit to the principle of the lease (whichever is earlier), while the ***commencement of the lease term*** is the date from which the lessee takes possession or begins to use the leased asset. Every lease provides for the **minimum lease payments**, which are the amounts the lessee is expected to pay over the lease term.

Recognition of a Lease

As stated above, a lease is recognized by its substance and not by the legal form of the agreement. The fact that an agreement uses the word "lease" does not automatically make such a transaction a lease agreement. Every agreement should be carefully evaluated to see if it conforms to the formal definition of a lease as stated above.

CLASSIFICATION OF LEASES

Leases are classified as either **finance lease** or **operating lease**. A **finance lease** is defined as "a lease that transfers all the risks and rewards incidental to ownership" of the leased asset to the lessee with or without the transfer of title. Any lease other than finance lease is to be classified as **operating lease**. These two classifications are especially important to your understanding of leases because each classification follows different accounting treatments.

The classification of a lease as either finance or operating, and the determination of amounts to be recognized at the commencement of the lease term (for finance lease) are done at **inception of the lease**.

LEASE MEASUREMENTS FOR LESSEES

Let us now turn our attention to the issue of measurements of finance and operating leases for both the **lessors** and the **lessees**.

Finance Lease

Under a finance lease, the lessee has acquired an asset; the lease arrangement only serves as an instrument for financing the acquisition of the asset. Thus, at the commencement of the lease term, the *lessee* shall recognize the lower of the **fair value** of the leased asset and the **present value** of the minimum lease payments (which comprises both the principal and finance charge) as asset and liability simultaneously. The discounting rate used in the calculation of present value should be the same as the interest rate in the lease agreement. All initial direct costs attributable to negotiating and arranging the lease are capitalized along with the leased asset as part of the initial measurement.

Subsequently, the lease payments shall be recognized. The lease payments, which should be apportioned between the repayment of outstanding liability and the finance charge, shall be recognized on a constant periodic basis with the finance charge allocated to profit or loss for each period.

Note that a finance lease often gives rise to noncurrent assets, which must be accounted for as Property, Plant and Equipment. The depreciation policy used should be consistent with that of the group which the asset belongs. The asset is to be depreciated over the shorter of its useful life and the lease term, with the resulting depreciation expense allocated to profit or loss.

Operating Leases

Under an operating lease, the lessee recognizes lease payments as an expense on a straight-line basis over the lease period (or term), or on any other basis that is more representative of the pattern of benefits the lessee derives from the leased assets. Lease expense, which excludes insurance and maintenance costs, is apportioned to profit or loss. The difference between the recognized lease expense and the actual payments made as at the reporting date is recognized as **operating lease asset or liability** in the Statement of Financial Position.

It is necessary to take note of special incentives such as interest-free or rent-free periods provided by the *lessor*. These incentives do not imply zero charge for the period; they are to be added to the entire lease so that the overall effect will result in reduced payments over the entire lease period.

LEASE MEASUREMENTS FOR LESSOR

Finance Lease Measurements

Having transferred all the rewards and risks of ownership of the leased assets to the lessee, the lessor shall, at the commencement date, derecognize the leased asset and recognize a **receivable** equal to the **net investment in the lease**. **Initial direct costs** (costs attributable to negotiating and arranging the lease) are included in the finance lease receivable.

Subsequent measurement of finance lease income is based on a systematic pattern that depicts constant periodic rate of returns on the leased asset over the lease term. **Lease receipts** (lessee's payments) are apportioned to the principal (leading to a reduction in lessee's debt) and to (unearned) finance income for the period.

For finance lease involving **manufacturer or dealer Lessors,** the transaction is treated as an outright sale, and this gives rise to the following income:

a) Initial recognition of **sales revenue** which is the minimum of either the fair value of the leased asset or the present value of minimum lease receipts based on market rate of interest.
b) Subsequent periodic recognition of **finance income** over the lease term.

Initial direct costs incurred because of arranging for the lease are recognized as expenses at the same time sales revenue is recognized. **Cost of sales** is the cost or carrying amount of the asset.

Operating Lease Measurements

In the case of operating lease, ownership of the leased asset remains with the lessor and the asset continues to be accounted for as *Property, Plant and Equipment* or as *Intangible Assets*.

The lessor shall recognize **lease income** from operating lease on a straight-line basis over the lease term or based on any other method that is more representative of the pattern of diminished benefit from the leased asset.

Costs incurred while earning the lease income (including depreciation on the leased assets) are recognized as expense. All initial direct costs incurred by the *lessors* are added to the carrying amount of the leased assets and recognized as expense over the lease term on the same periodic pattern as the lease income.

This pattern of income recognition also applies to manufacturer or dealer lessors. This is because operating lease cannot be recognized as sales since it does not transfer the risks and rewards of the leased assets to the lessee.

CHAPTER 3

CONSTRUCTION CONTRACTS

Standard revenue and expense recognitions apply to items of revenue (or expense) earned or incurred from transactions that begin and end within one accounting period. However, there are cases where a revenue (or expense)-generated transaction spans two or more accounting periods. Accounting for such items will require pro rata recognition of revenue and expense. Construction Contracts, which was previously a separate Standard (IAS 11), is now under **IFRS 15— Revenue from Contracts with Customers**.

WHAT IS A CONSTRUCTION CONTRACT?

A Construction Contract is defined by IFRS as "*a contract specifically negotiated for the construction of an asset or combination of assets that are closely interrelated or independent in terms of their design, technology or function.*"

When the start and completion dates of revenue (or expense) item to be accounted for span reporting periods, then such an item is accounted for as a construction Contract. The word "construction" can be interpreted to mean build, design, fabricate, create, develop, and thus making it possible to apply **Construction Contract** policies to services such as project management, software development, product marketing or promotion which could take more than one accounting year to complete. The construction of real estate should be accounted for in accordance with the Construction Contract.

Construction Contracts can be grouped into a **Fixed-priced contract** (where the contractor agrees to a fixed price or a fixed rate per specified measurable unit) or a **Cost-plus contract** (in which the contractor is reimbursed for all agreed and measurable costs plus a percentage of the costs or a fixed amount). Under both types of contracts, a customer can ask for a **variation** in the scope of work to be done (which may affect the cost of the contract either positively or negatively), and the contractor can make **claims** for additional amount with respect to cost not included in the original contract. Sometimes, a Construction Contract may include an option for **incentive payment** to the contractor if a specified standard or job completion date is met.

IAS 11 prescribes the criteria for the recognition of revenue and cost arising from Construction Contracts. It prescribes the rules on how to allocate revenue and cost to the accounting periods in which the construction occurred. Note that the Standard only applies to accounting in the financial statements of *contractors*; what happens at the customer's side of the transaction will depend on the type of asset being constructed or created.

CONTRACT REVENUE AND COST

Contract revenues comprise the **initial contract price** plus all subsequent **variations**, **claims** and **incentives**, while contract costs comprise of the following:

a) Direct cost (such as cost of materials, labour, depreciation on equipment, equipment hiring cost, etc.)
b) General contract overhead cost (such as warranty or insurance cost, cost for the transportation of materials and any overhead cost attributable to the contract)
c) Other costs (costs that are chargeable to the customer under the terms of the contract such as compensations and other claims from third parties).

Note that the recognition criteria for all aspects of revenues and costs arising from Construction Contract must satisfy part of **IFRS 15** requirements for the recognition of revenue and cost, namely, reliable measurement of revenue and cost. If it cannot be measured, then it cannot be recognized.

One contentious issue is whether costs incurred in the process of securing the contract should be included in the contract cost. Going by the provisions of the Standard such costs can only be included if they can be reliably measured and it is probable that the contract will be secured within the reporting period. However, if those pre-contract costs have already been expensed, then they cannot be reallocated to the contract no matter the circumstance.

Having identified what constitutes contract revenue and costs, let us briefly look at those items that are not recognized as costs under Construction Contracts. They include:

a) Selling and marketing costs.
b) General and administrative costs not specifically provided for reimbursement in the contract.
c) Non-reimbursable research and development costs.
d) Depreciation on plant and machinery not directly used in the execution of the contract.

Recognition of Contract Revenue and Expenses

IAS 11 provides the following criteria for the recognition of contract revenue and expenses in the income statement:

a) Revenue and costs associated with a construction contract can only be recognized when the outcome of the contract can be reliably measured.
b) Revenue and expenses shall be recognized by reference to the stage of completion of the contract activity at the balance sheet date.

When can a reliable estimate said to be obtained for the **outcome** of a construction contract? The first criterion is the general requirement of IFRS 15(Revenue): **when it is probable that the economic benefit of the contract will flow to the entity**. The following additional requirements apply for a **fixed-price** contract:

a) Reliable measurement of total contract revenue
b) Reliable estimate of both the cost to complete the contract, as well as the stage of completion at the balance sheet date.

For **cost-plus** contract, the only additional requirement is the identification and reliable measurement of all costs attributable to the contract whether specifically reimbursable or not.

Contract revenue and expenses are recognized based on **percentage-of-completion method**, which involves matching revenue with costs incurred with respect to the actual work done in reaching a specific completion stage. This is the only method permitted under IAS 11 for the recognition of contract revenues and expenses. The method, whereby contract revenue and expenses are recognized only after completion of contract (completed-contract method), is not allowed under IFRS.

In an event where it becomes likely that contract costs will exceed contract revenue, then the loss should be recognized immediately in the income statement irrespective of the stage of completion.

DETERMINATION OF PERCENTAGE OF COMPLETION

Reliable measurement of the stages of completion of a construction contract is very crucial for accurate determination of revenue and expenses to be recognized. Where a contract provides measurable job completion milestones as the basis for stages of completion, such milestones can be used as a basis for the recognition of contract revenue and expenses. Where such milestones do not exist, IAS 11 provides the following methods for the estimation of percentage completion for a contract, depending on the nature of the contract:

a) **The proportion of costs method**: This method matches the portion of costs incurred to date against the total contract cost, and recognizes revenue based on the percentage of total contract cost incurred against the total costs required to complete the contract. For example, if the total cost required to complete a forty thousand Dollar contract is twenty thousand Dollar, and if the total cost incurred as at the reporting date is five thousand Dollar, then the percentage of completion (which is 20%) can be computed as follows:

Total Contract Revenue		$40,000
Total Contract Cost		$20,000
Total Cost incurred (as at reporting date)		$5,000
Percentage Completion	(5,000/20,000) x 100	20%
Contract Revenue to be recognized (20% of total revenue) for the period	(20/100) *40,000	$8,000

b) Independent surveys and physical verification of the value of the actual work done can also be used to determine the percentage of work completed.

CONTRACT WORK IN PROGRESS

In many situations, it is advantageous to buy construction materials in bulk (more than the actual quantity required at a given moment) and deliver the materials to site to take advantage of volume discounts or future unfavourable price fluctuations. Costs for the portion of materials not yet used (those meant for future use) should be recognized as assets and classified under Contract Work in Progress. This cost should not be included in the total cost used for the computation of percentage completion for revenue recognition.

Note that the actual amount received for the contract is not equal to the amount recognized as revenue, as some receipts may include **advances**. All advances should be recognized as a **liability due to customers**. The total amount billed to customer for contract work carried out (whether paid or unpaid) called **Progress billings**, should be recognized as **asset due from customer**. Some contract may provide for **retention**—part of the contract amount that is withheld until certain conditions are met.

DISCLOSURE

The following disclosures, most of which are expected on the face of the financial statements, should form part of your financial statements or notes:

a) The amount of contract revenue recognized as revenue during the period should be disclosed in the Statement of Comprehensive Income, and the method used for revenue recognition and stage of completion should form part of the accounting policies disclosure.

b) The following disclosures are required in the Statement of Financial Position: total advances received, amount held as retention, total amount due to customer, total amount due from customer, and contract work in progress. Contingent assets and liabilities such as warranty and claims (in accordance with the relevant Standards) should also be disclosed.

CHAPTER 4

ACCOUNTING FOR THE CONSTRUCTION OF REAL ESTATE

Let us look at the issues and accounting policies that apply to an agreement or contract for the construction of real estate for residential, commercial, or industrial use. We will be considering the recognition and accounting for revenue and expense (or cost) with respect to the construction of real estate which spans two or more accounting period. Specifically, we will look at how to determine whether an agreement for the construction of real estate falls within the scope of **Construction Contracts** or **Revenue.**

ACCOUNTING TREATMENT

IFRIC 15 clarifies issues relating to the construction of real estate meant for residential, commercial, or industrial use. The interpretation applies to the entity (the contactor) handling the construction, and not the owner of the estate. Based on **IFRIC 15** (which has now been merged with other revenue-related Standards and Interpretations to become IFRS 16), the following accounting options apply to the recognition of revenue and expense for the **Agreement for the Construction of Real Estate**:

a) Treatment strictly in accordance with Construction Contracts
b) Treatment in accordance with Rendering of service
c) Treatment in accordance with Sale of goods

IFRIC 15 stipulates that if the agreement mandates the buyer (or owner of the project) to specify or modify the design of the major structural components of the project before or during the construction, then the agreement should be treated as a construction contract and must follow all the recognition rules and accounting treatment applicable to **Construction Contracts**.

However, when construction is carried out independent of the buyer and the buyer has little or no ability to influence the designs, then the agreement should be treated in accordance with **IFRS 15** (Revenue). Where revenue recognition falls within the scope of IFRS 15, then the criteria required for classifying the revenue either as "rendering of service" or "sale of goods" depend on whether the construction **materials** and **labour** are provided by the entity (the contractor) or the buyer.

a) If the entity handling the construction provides both the materials and labour for the construction, then the agreement is for the **sale of goods**, and revenue can only be recognized when the entity has transferred control and significant risks of ownership to the buyer.
b) Where the entity provides labour only, then the agreement is for the **rendering of service**, and revenue is recognized using the percentage-of-completion method.

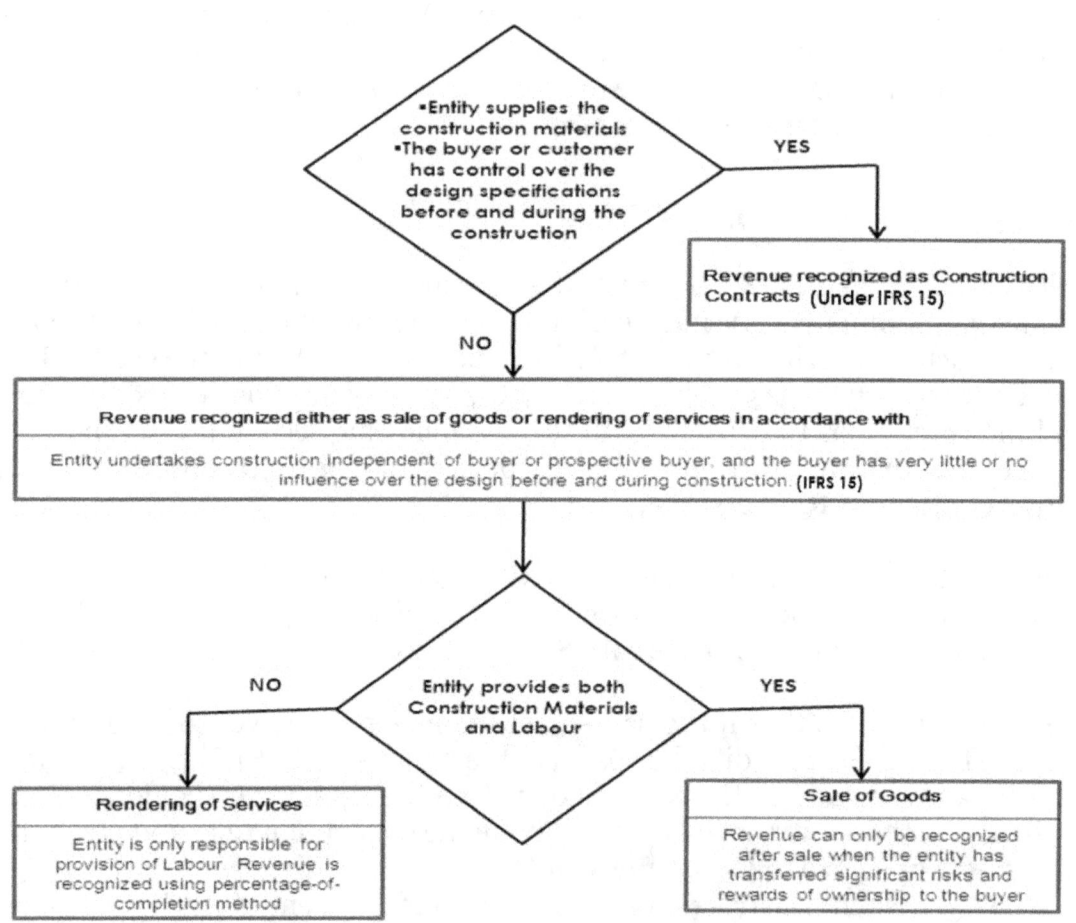

RECOGNITION OF TOTAL CONSTRUCTION COST

At the end of the construction, the owner of the property will have to recognize the total cost of the property. The debit side for the total cost will depend on the intended purpose of the property.

a) For owner-occupied property, total construction cost should be debited to **Property, Plant and Equipment (PPE).**
b) For property meant for sale, total construction cost should be debited to **Inventory.**
c) Where the resulting property is for operating lease, total construction cost should be debited to **Investment Property.**
d) The credit side of the transaction depends on the type of agreement that was used for the construction of the real estate.

1) **If the construction was accounted for as Construction Contract**
2) Here the buyer or owner paid for the cost of the construction based on the contractual agreement. The owner will therefore recognize this payment by crediting **Cash**.
3) **If the construction was accounted for as Sale of Goods**
4) Here the buyer simply pays for goods, and this involves crediting **Cash**.
5) **If the construction was accounted for as Rendering of Service**

Here the buyer was responsible for the materials used in the construction and only paid the contractor for labour. While the construction was going on all the construction costs (including materials and labour) were debited to Construction Work in Progress. On completion of the project, this cost must be transferred out by crediting **Construction Work in Progress**.

ACCOUNTING FOR REAL ESTATE AFTER CONSTRUCTION

Note that IFRIC 15 applies to the contractor during the construction phase of the property. On completion of the project, a different accounting policy will apply to the property. Note that a real estate entity can act as a contractor or a buyer/owner or both—depending on its role in the construction agreement and intended use of the property:

a) A real estate entity can be hired to construct real estate by another entity or individual (Contractor)

b) A real estate entity can hire a contractor for the construction of its own real estate (Owner or Buyer)
c) A real estate entity can undertake the construction of its own real estate (Contractor and Owner)

Whichever is the case, how the completed property is accounted for will be based on its actual or intended use, which falls into the following categories:

a) Owner-occupied
b) For sale
c) For lease

On completion, property can be accounted for using at least one of the following Standards, depending on its use or purpose:

- **IAS 16—Property, Plant and Equipment:** Properties that are constructed solely for use by the owner for domestic use or for conducting personal commercial or business activities should be accounted for in accordance with IAS 16—Property, Plant and Equipment.

- **IAS 2—Inventory:** Properties that are constructed sorely for sale should be accounted for in accordance with IAS 2—Inventory.

- **IAS 40—Investment Property:** Properties that are meant for rental or operating lease or capital appreciation should be accounted for in accordance with IAS 40—Investment Property.

SERVICE CONCESSION ARRANGEMENTS

It is becoming increasingly popular in many economies for government to enter into different forms of agreements with private sector operators for the provision of public services in exchange for rights to charge users of such public services. Examples include a concession arrangement with a private operator to develop (or upgrade), operate and maintain public infrastructure such as roads, airports, hospitals, etc. and charge fees for the use of these services by the public for an agreed number of years. The government exercises control over the type of services the operator must provide as well as the price and takes over the asset at the expiration of the contract. These types of arrangements may also go with such acronym as BOT (Build-Operate-Transfer).

IFRIC 12 (which is now a part of **IFRS 15**) was issued in response to the accounting challenges posed by such Service Concession arrangements. Specifically, IFRIC 12 provides guidelines on how a concession operator should apply existing IFRSs in accounting under service concession agreements. However, IFRIC 12 does not provide accounting treatment for the government (grantor) side of the arrangements.

IFRIC 12 recognizes two types of service concession as follows:

a) The first type is based on the **granting of financial assets**, while
b) The second type is the **granting of intangible assets**.

Granting of Financial Assets

Under this type of concession arrangement, the operator receives a financial asset in a form of *"an unconditional contractual right to receive a specified or determinable amount of cash or another financial asset from the government in return for constructing or upgrading a public-sector asset, and then operating and maintaining the asset for a specified period of time."* It also includes a provision that makes it mandatory for the grantor (government) to pay for any difference if the amounts received from users of the public service are less than the agreed amount.

Granting of Intangible Assets

Under this arrangement, the operator receives an intangible asset in a form of right or a license to charge the users for the use of public service provided. The operator has no unconditional right to receive cash as the amount received by the operator is contingent on the extent to which the services it provides are used by the public. Note that it is possible for both types of arrangement to co-exist in one contract, and IFRIC 12 permits such an arrangement.

System implementation should focus on the different accounting treatments that apply to the two types of concession arrangements. In the first arrangement, the operator recognizes a Financial Asset (and accounts for it in accordance with Financial Instruments), while in the second arrangement the operator recognizes Intangible Asset (and accounts for it in accordance with IAS 38—Intangible Asset). Neither of these arrangements allows the operator to recognize the infrastructure it develops and maintains as its own assets (Property, Plant and Equipment—IAS 16). Revenue and costs arising from construction, upgrade, and maintenance services under both arrangements should be recognized and measured in accordance with Revenue and Construction Contracts.

CHAPTER 5

PROPERTY, PLANT AND EQUIPMENT

Property, Plant and Equipment (PPE) is what was formerly referred to as **Fixed Assets** and is accounted for by the IFRS Standard **IAS 16**. PPE is classified under the group, Noncurrent Assets. Other items in this group include:

1) Intangible Assets (IAS 38)
2) Investment Property (IAS 40)
3) Noncurrent Assets Held for Sale (IFRS 5)
4) Biological agricultural assets (IAS 41)
5) Evaluation of mineral rights and reserves (IFRS 6)

Most of what was known as Fixed Asset is now classified as **Property, Plant and Equipment**. However, the term Fixed Asset is still being used for classification under IFRS for SMEs. So, we might be using the two terms interchangeably here.

   IAS 16 has prescribed the rules for the recognition, initial and subsequent measurements, as well as the disclosure requirements for Property, Plant and Equipment. IAS 16 does not cover those items already accounted for by other Standards, such as:

a) Investment Property
b) Noncurrent Assets Held for Sale (IFRS 5)
c) Biological agricultural assets (IAS 41)
d) Evaluation of mineral rights and reserves (IFRS 6)

RECOGNITION AND MEASUREMENT PARAMETERS

Property, Plant and Equipment (PPE) can be defined as **"*tangible assets that are held for use in production or for supply of goods and services, for rentals or for administrative purposes*" and are expected to be used for more than one accounting period**.

   The recognition criteria for PPE are as follows:

a) It is probable that future economic benefits embodied in the asset will flow into the entity controlling the asset.
b) The cost of the asset can be reliably measured.

Below are the definitions of some of the key terms associated with Property, Plant and Equipment:

Asset Cost

The amount paid to acquire or construct the asset. Asset cost comprises of the following:

a) Purchase or construction cost (including taxes, import duties, discounts, etc.)
b) Transportation, handling, and other charges incurred in the process of bringing the asset to location where it will be used.
c) Installation, set up and other costs directly attributable to bringing the asset to the state whereby it can be used as intended.

The following costs are excluded:

a) Operational and administrative overhead costs not directly attributable to acquisition of the asset
b) Advertising and promotional costs
c) Training costs

Useful Life

This is the length of time the asset is expected to be used (usually in years) or number of production units expected from use of the asset.

Residual Value

This is the estimated disposal (sale) amount, minus cost to sell, of the asset at the end of its useful life.

Depreciable Amount

This is the cost of the asset less its residual value. This is the amount that is depreciated:

- **Depreciable Amount = Asset Cost – Residual Value**

Depreciation

This is the periodic allocation of wear and tear on the asset as cost to the expense account over the useful life of the asset. This allocation could be on monthly or yearly basis. The sum of all the periodic depreciation, up to any given time, is called **accumulated depreciation**.

Sometimes, depreciation is specified by yearly **depreciation rate**, which is a constant value representing percentage of the depreciable amount to be charged as depreciation expense.

One important issue about depreciation is the method of depreciation used. Some of the permitted methods include:

a) Straight-line
b) Reducing-balance
c) Sum-of-the-year's digits

The **straight-line** method of depreciation, which apportions depreciation equally over each year (or each production unit) of the asset's service life, remains the most popular method of depreciation.

Entities are free to select any method of depreciation, but any method selected must match the pattern of usage or consumption of the item. The same method must be used for all the items within the same class. Note that IFRS prohibits the selection of accounting policies based on tax considerations. This also applies to the selection of depreciation method.

Carrying Amount

The **carrying amount** of an asset, also called **net book value** (NBV), is the asset **cost** less **accumulated depreciation** (and impairment losses—if any):

- Carrying Amount = Cost – Accumulated Depreciation – Impairment Loss

Fair Value

This is the amount at which the asset can be sold or exchanged between knowledgeable and willing parties in a formal, neutral, and unbiased transaction. Fair value reflects the true value of the asset.

Recoverable Amount

This is the asset's **net selling price** or its **value in use**—whichever is higher. **Impairment**.

   Impairment loss is the amount by which the carrying amount of an asset exceeds its recoverable amount. Impairment of assets is extensively covered as a separate Standard under IAS 36.

MEASUREMENTS

Initial Measurement

On recognition, an item of PPE shall be measured at the total of what it costs to acquire the asset with the following accounting entries:

> Dr.   Asset Cost
> Cr.   Cash/Creditor

At this point, accumulated depreciation is zero. However, the **depreciable amount** is computed as: ***Asset Cost – Residual Value***

Subsequent Measurements

For subsequent measurements, there are two models to choose from: **Cost** or **Revaluation** model.

- **Cost Model**
  The **Cost** model (also called **depreciation model**) involves the systematic apportionment of a specified amount (based on depreciation method used) representing a part of the original cost as depreciation expense over the life of the asset, using a known depreciation method.
      The following accounting entries must accompany each depreciation measurement:

  Depreciation
  > □   Dr.   Depreciation Expense A/C
  > □   Cr.   Accumulated Depreciation A/C

After depreciation, the **carrying amount** of each asset, measured under the cost model, must be recomputed as follows:

Carrying Amount = Asset Cost – Accumulated Depreciation

- **Revaluation Model**
The revaluation method requires physical revaluation of the asset (or class of assets) at regular intervals to obtain a new value for the asset based on their fair values. Any gain arising from revaluation should be recognized in Other Comprehensive Income (Equity) under the heading "Revaluation Surplus", while losses should be recognized as expense in Profit or Loss. Below is the summary of accounting entries for revaluation gain or loss:

Gain: Carrying Amount - Revalued Amount > 0

- □ Dr.Asset Cost A/C
- □ Cr. Revaluation Surplus (Other Comprehensive Income under Equity)

A reversal of an earlier increase for the same asset should be debited to *Other Comprehensive Income.*

Loss: Carrying Amount - Revalued Amount < 0 or Revalued Amount – Carrying Amount > 0

- □ Dr.   Revaluation Loss (Profit or Loss) A/C
- □ Cr.   Asset Cost A/C

NOTE

a) A reversal of an earlier loss for the same asset should be credited to *Profit or Loss.*
b) Revaluation surplus may be released to Retained Earnings when the asset is derecognized or disposed. On no account should revaluation surplus be credited to Profit or Loss.

COMPONENTIZATION

Componentization policy simply states that **component parts of an item of property, plant and equipment with different useful lives or depreciation rates and with costs that are significant, in relation to the total cost, must be depreciated separately**. However, what is considered "significant" is left to judgment (some jurisdictions may consider anything from 5% as being significant).

Componentization is one challenging issue for entities converting from GAAP to IFRS as there may be no sufficient information for the componentization of existing assets.

CHANGES IN ESTIMATES

IFRS require that both the **useful lives**, **residual values** and **depreciation methods** of items of property, plants and equipment should be reviewed annually, and the estimates adjusted whenever necessary based on prevailing realities and circumstances. For example, the residual value of an item can be adjusted upward if existing market indicators suggest so. These adjustments are regarded as changes in estimates and do not warrant any accounting entry since they are not correction of errors. However, they will affect the **carrying amount** of the asset in the current and future periods only.

IMPAIRMENTS

Impairment loss is defined as **the amount by which the carrying amount of an asset exceeds its recoverable amount** (*recoverable amount* is the higher of net selling price and value in use).

Yearly impairment testing is mandatory for some class of assets. You are expected to collate yearly schedule of impairment losses and make appropriate adjustments to assets carrying values and depreciation charges based on these losses. Provision should also be made for the reversal of impairment losses (except for *Goodwill*) and the readjustment of the carrying values and depreciation charges for the affected assets.

The following accounting entries apply to impairment loss:

- □ Dr. Impairment Loss (Profit or Loss)
- □ Cr. Asset Cost

COMPONENT REPLACEMENT OR UPGRADE

Routine repairs and maintenance costs for items of property, plant and equipment are written off as expense. However, when a major component of the asset involving a significant cost is replaced then the cost can be capitalized. Such capitalization can only be allowed under the following conditions: **if the cost of**

the replaced component was separately identified on initial recognition and it is evident that the replacement will result in more economic benefits.

If there is no data to determine the cost of the replaced component, then the replacement cost can be used to determine the initial cost of the replaced component by discounting back to its present value at the time of initial recognition. This value has to be taken out of the book before adding the cost of the replaced component.

It is obvious that replacing the engine of a car will definitely result in more economic benefits, at least in terms of performance and reduction in repairs and maintenance costs. However, the cost of the engine and the chassis of a car are not usually quoted separately on purchase. But the cost of replacing the engine meets the requirement for capitalization.

Assuming the car was bought for $40,000 five years ago, and the cost of the replaced engine is $5,000. Using appropriate discounting rate, we can determine approximate cost of the engine five years ago, when the car was bought, through its Present Value (P) using the formula:

$$P = \frac{A}{(1+i)}n$$

(where A is the future amount i the discount rate and n the number of years).

Based on this formula, (if we take 10% as the discount rate) the cost of the engine five years ago when the car was initially purchased can be computed as **$5,000/ (1+0.1) ^5 = $3,105.59**. This amount must be taken out of the book through the following accounting entries:

Discounted Cost of the Engine ($3,105.59):

- ☐ Dr.Accumulated Depreciation
- ☐ Cr. Asset Cost

The cost of the new component ($5,000) should be added to the book, by passing the following entries:

Actual Cost of the New Engine ($5,000)
- ☐ Dr.Asset Cost
- ☐ Cr. Cash/Debtor

Make appropriate adjustment in the asset register and ensure that the new carrying amount of the asset comes to **41,894.41** (40,000 − 3,105.59 + 5,000).

DERECOGNITION

An item of property, plants and equipment shall be derecognized when no further economic benefit is expected from its use or when the asset is disposed. This can also happen when any one of the following events occurs:

a) Sale or write-off
b) Transfer to another class, for example from PPE to Inventory or Investment Property.

Depreciation ceases on de-recognition.

Gain on disposal shall not be recognized in the income statement, except for an entity that routinely sells such items as part of its normal business activities. However, such items of property, plant and equipment must first be reclassified as held for sale (IFRS 5) before the actual sale.

Some of the accounting entries that should accompany de-recognitions are as follows:

Sale

- **Original Asset Cost:**
  - ☐ Dr. Asset Disposal
  - ☐ Cr. Asset Cost

- **Accumulated Depreciation:**
  - ☐ Dr. Accumulated Depreciation
  - ☐ Cr. Asset Disposal

- **Selling Price:**
  - ☐ Dr. Cashbook (or Debtor)
  - ☐ Cr. Asset Disposal

- **Profit or Loss**

  Profit
  - ☐ Dr. Asset Disposal
  - ☐ Cr. Disposal Income or Other Comprehensive Income

<u>Loss</u>
- ☐ Dr. Disposal Expense (Profit or Loss)
- ☐ Cr. Asset Disposal

Write-Off

Two cases are possible here:

(a) When the carrying amount is equal to zero
This means the asset has served out its useful life. The following book entries apply:

<u>Accumulated Depreciation</u>

- ☐ Dr. Accumulated Depreciation
- ☐ Cr. Asset Cost

(b)   When the carrying amount is not equal to zero
Here the asset is either damaged beyond restoration or is stolen while still in use. The following accounting entries apply:

<u>Carrying Amount</u>
- ☐ Dr. Asset Write-off
<u>Accumulated Depreciation</u>
- ☐ Dr. Accumulated Depreciation
<u>Carrying Amount + Accumulated Depreciation</u>
- ☐ Cr. Asset Cost

ALTERNATIVE METHODS

SALE

<u>Original Asset Cost</u>
Cr. Asset Cost Account

<u>Accumulated Depreciation</u>
Dr. Accumulated Depreciation Account

<u>Selling Price</u>
Dr. Cash (or Debtor) Account

<u>Profit</u>
Cr. Asset Disposal Account
OR

<u>Loss</u>
Dr. Asset Disposal Account

WRITE-OFF

<u>Original Asset Cost</u>
Cr. Asset Cost Account

<u>Accumulated Depreciation</u>
Dr. Accumulated Depreciation Account

<u>Carrying Amount</u>
Dr. Asset Disposal Account

Transfer of Asset

Assets are transferred at their carrying amount. The following accounting entries apply to transfer of asset:

<u>Carrying Amount</u>
- □ Dr.   Destination Asset Cost
- □ Cr.   Source Asset Cost

<u>Accumulated Depreciation</u>
- □ Dr.   Accumulated Depreciation
- □ Cr.   Source Asset Cost

CHAPTER 6

INVESTMENT PROPERTY

Investments in lands and buildings have become one of the dominant activities in all economies. Investment Property belongs to the group of assets classified as noncurrent assets—just like Property, Plant and Equipment. However, investment properties are different by the fact that they generate cash flows independently and, thus, require different accounting treatments. This chapter looks at the IFRS classification, recognition, measurements, and disclosure requirements for investment property.

IAS 40 prescribes the rules and criteria for the recognition, measurements, and the disclosure requirements for **Investment Property.** But first, we need to formally define Investment Property to enable us to know those items that should be classified as Investment Property.

WHAT IS INVESTMENT PROPERTY?

Investment property is defined as *land or building or both held by the owner for the purpose of earning rental income or for capital appreciation or both—rather than for use in the production or supply of goods and services, or for sale in the ordinary course of business.*

One distinctive feature of an investment property is that it generates cash flows independently. Thus, owner-occupied property cannot be classified as an Investment Property. However, when an entity leases out a part of the building and occupies a part, the property can only be classified as investment property if:

a) The leased portion can be sold separately or
b) The occupied portion is insignificant.

But what is considered "insignificant" is a matter of judgment. Some jurisdictions may consider anything less than 10% as insignificant.

IAS 40 applies to all investment property under the following financial conditions:

a) Lessees' financial statements held under a **finance lease.**
b) Lessors' financial statements under an **operating lease**.

IAS 40 does not apply to a lessee's financial statement for a property under an operating lease. Properties that are covered by other Standards are also excluded from investment property. See Chapter 9 for detailed discussion on Leases.

CLASSIFICATION AND MEASUREMENTS OF INVESTMENT PROPERTY

Classification

Since investment properties are likely to coexist with other groups of noncurrent assets our first task has to do with proper classification of investment property to avoid mistakes or mix-up when applying the relevant policy.

Investment properties that are held for sale in the ordinary course of business should be classified as inventory and accounted for in accordance with **IAS 2** (and not IFRS 5—Noncurrent Assets Held for Sale); while owner-occupied properties should be classified as Property, Plant and Equipment and accounted for in accordance with **IAS 16**.

Measurements

On recognition as an asset, an investment property is measured at cost (including transaction charges). For subsequent measurement, an entity shall choose either the cost model or the fair value (revaluation) model for all its investment property. However, if a property held under operating lease is classified as investment property, then the entity (lessor) must select the fair value model for all its investment property. Any gains or losses resulting from change in fair value of an investment property shall be recognized in profit or loss.

Entities implementing IAS 40 should also take note of the following provisions:

a) When an investment property is measured at fair value, it shall continue to be measured at fair value until disposal even if there is no reliable market data.
b) If an investment property cannot be measured on a continuing basis using fair value, then the property shall be measured using the cost model until disposal.
c) If an entity decides to use the cost model for its investment property, then all of its investment property shall be measured in accordance with IAS 16

(Property, Plant and Equipment), except those classified as held-for-sale (which fall under IFRS 5).

Transfers

Transfers to and from investment property shall be carried out whenever there is a change of use. Some of the possible scenarios include:

a) From owner-occupied to investment property
b) From investment property to property, plant, and equipment (IAS 16)
c) From inventories to investment property

Any change arising from fair value re-measurement on transfer shall be recognized in profit or loss.

Disposal

An investment property shall be derecognized when no more economic benefits are expected from it, or on disposal. Any gain or loss on disposal shall be recognized in profit or loss.

Most of the accounting entries that accompany measurements, transfers and disposal are like those of property, plant, and equipment under IAS 16 .

RECOGNITION OF RENTAL INCOME

In addition to the measurement policies for the investment property which apply to lessee (for investment property under finance lease) and lessor (for investment property under operating lease), **rental income** from the property will have to be recognized in accordance with IAS 18:

Initial Measurement (Recognition of Unearned Income on commencement of contract)

If the contract stipulates that rent be paid in advance, then on commencement of the contract the following accounting entries apply:

Invoice for the Period

- ☐   Dr.   Tenant
- ☐   Cr.   Unearned (or Accrued) Income

Subsequent Measurement (Recognition of Rental Income)

Recognize monthly rental income at the end or beginning of each month or period (as stipulated in the agreement):

- ☐ Dr.   Unearned Income
- ☐ Cr.   Rental Income (Profit or Loss)

Monthly recognition of income continues until Unearned Income balance is zero, or until the (lease) contract expires.

Receipt

When the tenant makes payment, the following accounting entries apply:

- ☐ Dr.   Cash/Bank
- ☐ Cr.   Tenant

NOTE

Cash receipt may or may not coincide with the recognition of income, and even if the two events take place simultaneously, the entries above must still be carried out to satisfy the requirement for accrual-basis accounting.

DISCLOSURE

The disclosure requirements for investment property are quite extensive and entails elaborate documentation and accurate record keeping. Where relevant documentation does not exist, the first step will be to compile and build investment asset register from available data. Some of the important data that should be found in such a register must include:

a) Detailed description of each property
b) Measurement model used (whether cost or fair value), and if cost model is used indicate the **depreciation method**, **useful life** or **depreciation rate** used for each property.
c) Carrying amount of each property and the effective date.
d) Gross annual rental income for each property.
e) Annual operating expense for each property.

This basic data can be used as a starting point for detailed IAS 40 disclosures.

The following disclosures are expected on the face of Statement of Comprehensive Income:

a) Rental income from investment property.
b) Direct operating expenses that generate rental income.
c) Direct operating expenses that did not generate rental income.

Some of the disclosures that are required as notes include:

a) The accounting policies—measurement bases and model (cost or fair value); circumstances under which fair-valued property interests under operating leases are classified as investment property; the criteria used to distinguish investment property from owner-occupied property and property held for sale in the ordinary course of business.
b) The methods and significant assumptions used in determining fair value.
c) Whether fair values are based on assessments by independent and qualified Valuers or not.

It is not possible to list all the disclosure requirements for IAS 40 here; entities implementing this Standard are advised to refer to IASB's Standards publications for detailed list of all the disclosures.

One important thing to take note of is the fact that although IAS 40 provides two options—cost or fair value - for the measurement of investment properties, it also makes it mandatory for entities to disclose the fair value amount of their investment properties (irrespective of whether the cost or fair value model used). For this reason, periodic property revaluation is mandatory even if the entity uses cost model for all its investment properties.

CHAPTER 7

INVENTORIES

Many businesses maintain stock (or inventory) of goods for one or all of the following reasons:

a) For sale
b) As raw materials to produce other goods
c) For use in the provision of services.

The major accounting issues with Inventory involve appropriate calculation of cost and the recognition of revenue and expenses associated with sales. One additional issue to be considered is **inventory write-down**. IAS 2 is the Standard that prescribes the criteria for accounting treatment of Inventories.

A manufacturing entity starts by building raw materials inventory and later transfer the materials to Work-in-Progress inventory before coming out with the finished products inventory; but a retail trader who simply buys goods for resale has no need for this transformation. We have already encountered the transformation that takes place with respect to the construction of real estate in the previous chapter.

WHAT IS INVENTORY?

IAS 2 defines inventories as assets that are:

a) Held as raw materials to be used in the production of goods or provision of services.
b) In the process of being transformed to goods (also called Work-in-progress).
c) In the form of finished products or goods held for sale in the ordinary course of business.

IAS 2 does not apply to materials or inventory already covered by other Standards such as agricultural produce (which is covered by IAS 41) or Construction Contracts Work in progress (which comes under IAS 11).

INVENTORY COSTS AND COSTING METHODS

Inventory costs comprise the following:

a) Cost of purchase (including taxes, import duties, transportation, and handling charges, etc.).
b) Production or conversion costs, which include all direct costs and overhead costs attributable to converting the raw materials to finished goods.

The following costs are excluded:

a) Raw materials wastage
b) Non-production storage costs
c) Overhead costs not directly attributable to the production of the item
d) Selling costs such as advertising and promotion

Cost accounting is a major topic in accounting and is beyond the scope of this book.

NET REALIZABLE VALUE (NRV)

Net Realizable Value (NRV) is the **estimated selling price** less the **total estimated transaction costs**.

INVENTORY COSTING METHODS (COST FLOW)

Inventories are measured or valued at the lower of **cost** and **net realizable value**. When the inventory items have uniform properties and are interchangeable, one of the following methods can be used to determine the cost of individual items as new items are added to the inventory:

a) **First-In-First-Out (FIFO)**
b) **Weighted average**

In FIFO, it is assumed that items are sold according to the order in which they were purchased or produced (from first to last). The weighted average costing method re-computes a new cost for each item whenever new items are added by computing the weighted average of the new and old items.

If, for example, there were 100 items valued at $250 each before the arrival of a new batch of 50 new units of the same items valued at $225 each, under FIFO it is assumed that the 100 items that were originally in stock will be sold before the 50 new items. But using the weighted average method the new cost for each of the 150 items can be computed as follows:

$$\text{Cost} = \frac{100x250 + 50x225}{100 + 50} = 241.67$$

These two are the only cost measurement methods allowed under IFRS, other measurement methods, such as Last-In-First-Out (LIFO) are not allowed.

INVENTORIES WRITE-DOWN

Under IFRS, it is strictly recommended that assets should not be carried at amounts that are likely to be higher than their sale or fair values. This is to ensure that "toxic" assets are eliminated from the books, to prevent using such assets as a camouflage to deceive investors.

There are many situations that can impact negatively on the carrying value of assets, and they include:

a) Damages
b) Obsolescence
c) Decline in selling price.

Whenever any of these events becomes obvious, it is necessary to write-down the value of the inventory to its net realizable value (NRV). Write-down is carried out for each item.

All losses incurred because of inventory write-down should be recognized as expense in the period that the write-down occurred. *Write-down* loss can be reversed if the condition later becomes favourable. Any amount incurred because of reversal should be recognized as a reduction in the loss recorded for previous write-down within the same period.

Write-down estimates must reflect the purpose for which the inventories are held. For example, inventories that are held for sale should be *written down* against the prevailing market prices, but inventories that are held for servicing sales contract should be written down against contract prices. You may require the services of an expert to write-down inventories in the absence of good software.

STANDARD ACCOUNTING ENTRIES ASSOCIATED WITH INVENTORY

- **SALE**

  When inventories are sold revenue is recognized along with the related cost simultaneously. The accounting entries are as follows:

  Selling Price
  - □ Dr. Cash (or Receivable)
  - □ Cr. Sales Revenue

  Cost Price
  - □ Dr. Cost of Sales
  - □ Cr. Inventory

- **PURCHASE**

  Cost Price
  - □ Dr. Inventory
  - □ Cr. Cash (Payable)

  Remember to re-compute the cost price of each item using any of the two recommended costing methods.

- **WRITE-DOWN**

  Write-down Losses
  - □ Dr. Inventory Write-down Loss
  - □ Cr. Inventory

- **WRITE-DOWN REVERSAL**

Write-down Gains
- □ Dr. Inventory
- □ Cr. Inventory Write-down Loss

■ **TRANSFERS**

In a production process, raw materials are transferred to work in progress and from work in progress to finished goods before they are sold. All such transfers are carried out at cost:

Cost
- □ Dr. Target or Destination Inventory
- □ Cr. Source Inventory

MANUAL INVENTORY UPDATES

Apart from Sales and Purchases which update the inventory directly, it might be necessary to manually adjust inventory due to several reasons. One good example is when some items are damaged or have expired. Such items must be manually removed from stock. In this situation, both the *Inventory Register* and inventory movement (*Inventory Journal*) must be updated manually. However, for the General Ledger entries, the items must be written off at cost with the following entries:

- □ Dr.   Cost of Sales (or Inventory Write-off Expense)
- □ Cr.   Inventory

THE INVENTORY REGISTER

Irrespective of whether you are managing your inventory manually or with automated system, a good inventory register is a must. While the accounting entries are posted to the General Ledger, your inventory register must keep accurate details of the quantity of each item in stock as well as the *in* and *out* movements of each item.

The basic data fields that are required in the inventory register are as follows:

- □ Item Code (unique for each item)
- □ Item Description
- □ Item Class or Category
- □ Unit Cost Price

- ☐ Unit Selling Price
- ☐ Unit of Measure
- ☐ Quantity in Stock
- ☐ Re-order Quantity
  - ○ .
  - ○ .
- ☐ Inventory Account Code
- ☐ Sales Account Code
- ☐ Cost of Sales Account Code
  - ○ .
  - ○ .
- ☐ Last Update Date

There may be need for additional fields, depending on the implementation, but these are just the basic ones. It is important to group items into defined classes or categories in the register, and associate each item to existing inventory, sale, and cost sale accounts in the Chart of Accounts.

CHAPTER 8

FINANCIAL INVESTMENT CALCULATIONS FOR REAL ESTATE

Real Estate business can involve several portfolios of investments both in the inward and outward directions. A real estate firm that borrows money from the bank to finance the construction of real estate must deal with the issue of interest payment as well as expected returns on the investment. Some of the analyses to be carried to make a safe decision may involve mathematical computations that are not so obvious and common to the average person in the industry. However, many may be familiar with some of the names, but not with the mathematics behind them:

- Future Value
- Sinking Fund Factor (SFF) and Sinking
- Present Value
- Annuity
- Internal Rate of Returns (IRR)
- Discounted Cash Flow
- Mortgage Loan Payment Schedule

In this chapter, we want to deal with the mathematics and the computations behind some of these analyses. In order not to scare some people away, we will simply state the formula and explain how they can be applied and leave out the mathematical derivations that give rise to these formulas.

FUTURE VALUE

The **Future Value** answers the question: *If I invest a certain amount of money today, how much will it yield in the future, (say 1 or 2 years* *later), based on a given interest rate?* We will look at three different investment scenarios that provide answers to this question.

Simple Interest

Now, let **P** denote the amount invested (Principal or Present Value), and let **r**(%) denote the interest rate for a period **n** (years). If **I** is the interest accrued within the period, the Future Value (**FV**), which is *Principal plus Interest*, can be stated as:

$$FV = P + I$$

We can calculate the interest earned (**I**), using the formula, known as the *Simple Interest*, as follows:

$$I = Prn$$

If we substitute for I in the first equation and rearrange the variables, we arrive at the following formula for Future Value:

$$FV = P(1 + rn)$$

Note:

a) r is the fixed annual interest rate. If, for example, the interest rate is 10%, r=0.1

b) n is the duration in years. If the duration is stated in months, then becomes.

$$\frac{n}{12}$$

Example 1: *If you invest $2,000 for 9 months at an annual interest rate of 12% (0.12), your FV at the end of the 9 months (0.75 year) will be $2,725, as shown below:*

$$FV = 2,500[1 + (0.12)(0.75)] = 2,500(0.09) = 2,725$$

If this same amount is invested for one year, the return at the end of one year will be $2,800.

Compound Interest

What we have done so far is based on a simple (straight line) interest, based on a fixed principal. In practice, most investments of this nature are based on what is called Compound Interest. Under compound Interest, the interest earned during the previous period is added to the *Principal*, and interest for the next period is computed based on the new *Principal*. This process is continuous throughout the tenure of the investment.

Another key factor to take note of here is that interest was computed only at the end of the period. Under Compound Interest regime, interest is computed and compounded periodically (monthly, quarterly, weekly, or even daily) based on agreed terms. So, the formula for Compound Interest introduces what is called compounding intervals (m).

Thus, the Future Value formula for an investment (P), for a period of n years @ a fixed annual interest rate r, compounded m times a year, is as follows:

$$FV = P\left(1 + \frac{r}{m}\right)^{mn}$$

If the compounding interval is once a year (m=1), this formula becomes:

$$FV = P(1 + r)^n$$

In using this formula, remember once again: r is in percentage and should be divided by 100, and if n is given in months, you should divide n by 12.

Example 2: *If we invest the same amount used in the previous example for one year, compounded monthly (12 times a year), the result will be as follows (r = 12% (0.12); n = 1 Year; m = 12):*

$$FV = 2{,}500\left(1 + \frac{0.12}{12}\right)^{12} = 2{,}500(1.01)^{12} = 2{,}500(1.1268) = 2{,}817$$

Note that this investment is only for one year. If however, the amount is invested for 2 years (24 compounding periods), the FV value will be as follows:

$$FV = 2{,}500\left(1 + \frac{0.12}{12}\right)^{2 \times 12} = 2{,}500(1.01)^{24} = 2{,}500(1.2697) = 3{,}174.25$$

But if this same amount is compounded once a year, the result for the two years will be as follows:

$$FV = 2,500 \left(1 + \frac{0.12}{1}\right)^2 = 2,500(1.01)^2 = 2,500(1.2544) = 3,136$$

From these examples, we can see that the more the compounding periods the higher the future value. The difference may appear so insignificant, but when the amount invested is large, the difference can be huge.

Annuity

In each of the two scenarios above, we are dealing with a fixed sum (P) invested over a given period n @ a fixed interest rate r (compounded m times a year). However, there is another scenario where a fixed sum (P) is invested every month (or year) successively for n years @ a fixed interest rate of r% compounded m times a year. In this case, instead of a fixed one-time investment, we have a fixed amount added to the investment every month or year, to yield a future sum, based on agreed interest rate. This is what is referred to as **annuity.** Annuity answers the question: ***If I keep depositing a fixed amount of money every month for one or more years, how much will it yield, based on a specified compound interest rate, at the end of its tenure?***

Computing the Future Value for this type of investment involves computing the Future Value for each period using the formula above and summing up the result for the duration of the investment. This summing up process is represented by the series:

$$FVA = P\left(1 + \frac{i}{x}\right)^1 + P\left(1 + \frac{i}{x}\right)^2 + P\left(1 + \frac{i}{x}\right)^3 + P + \ldots\ldots\left(1 + \frac{i}{x}\right)^{mn-1} + P$$

Using the summation sign, this series can be compressed to obtain a compact formula for a repeated investment of a fixed sum, **P**, made every **x** time a year, over a period **n** year @ **r**% interest, compounded **m** times a year:

$$FVA = P\sum_{t=1}^{n.m-1}\left(1 + \frac{i}{x}\right)^t + P$$

If the investment or deposit interval is yearly, x=1; if it is monthly, x=12; if it is quarterly, x=4; if it is weekly, x=52; if it is daily, x=365.

One form of this formula is the one where the repeated payments is a monthly instalment over a period of **n** years, compounded yearly @ **i**% interest rate. That means x=12 and m=1, reducing the formula to:

$$FVA = P \sum_{t=1}^{n.-1} \left(1 + \frac{i}{12}\right)^t + P$$

If the annuity (recurrent deposits) is yearly and the compounding is done at the end of every year, then the formula becomes simpler:

$$FVA = P \sum_{t=1}^{n.-1} (1 + i)^t + P$$

This is, perhaps the popular form of this equation—the one most people are familiar with.

Example 3: Let us consider the Future Value for a yearly annuity of $2,500 at annual interest rate of 10% over a period of 4 years, compounded yearly. Using the formula:

$$FVA = P \left(1 + \frac{i}{x}\right)^1 + P \left(1 + \frac{i}{x}\right)^2 + P \left(1 + \frac{i}{x}\right)^3 + P + \ldots \ldots \left(1 + \frac{i}{x}\right)^{mn-1} + P$$

We have,

$$FVA = 2,500(1 + 0.1)^1 + 2,500(1 + 0.1)^2 + 2500(1 + 0.1)^3 + 2,500$$
$$FVA = 2,500(1.1)^1 + 2,500(1.1)^2 + 2500(1.1)^3 + 2,500 = \mathbf{11,602.50}$$

At the end of four years, the investor will receive $11,602.50.

PRESENT VALUE

Future Value is about using what we know in the present to determine what happens in the future. Now, we are going to examine the opposite: using what we know (or expect) about the future to determine its equivalent in the present. In calculating the future value, we walk from the known (the present) to the future (unknown), but in calculating the present value, our known variable is the future, while the present is the unknown we are out to find.

The **Present Value (PV)**, answers the question: ***If I know what an investment will fetch in the future, what is the worth or value of that investment today?*** This is walking from the future back to the present. To enable us to take that walk, we must introduce what is called "discounting rate." Discounting rate is like the interest rate, but it acts in the opposite direction.

To understand the difference between **Present Value** and **Future Value**, look at it this way: *For Future Value, you are the client making payments to an investor to get a future sum. However, in the case of Present Value, see yourself as an investor collecting money from, representing the Present Value of a known future return from an investment, from a client.* Also, in this regard, instead of using the term "**compounding period**," we will be using, "**conversion period**." This is how frequent the future sum is discounted.

When you deposit money in the bank, you are looking forward to the future value of what you have invested, but when you borrow money from the bank, what the bank is charging you presently is based on the future value of that money, which is known to the bank (or fixed by the bank). In real estate transactions, Present Value-related transactions play out more often, in the form of borrowing money to finance real estate projects, as well as selling the properties on mortgage or under short-term financing.

Under the Future Value scenario, we have an individual or investor who has money to tie down for n years, either by making a one-time deposit or through series of periodic payments, to obtain a future sum. On the other hand, in the case of Present Value, we have an individual who needs either a lump sum of money now, or series of periodic receipts over a period of years.

Present Value of a One-time Investment

Under the Future Value scenario, we have an individual or investor who has money to tie down for n years by making a one-time deposit to obtain a future sum. However, with Present Value, you have an investor who wants to pay today for an investment that will return a future sum. The investor will pay a discounted price for the future sum expected from this investment.

We do not have any new formula for Present Value calculations. If you examine all the formulas we have used so far in calculating Future Value, the P in these formulas represents the *Present Value*. So, to obtain the formula for Present Value (PV), all we need to do is to make **P** the subject of these formulas. Doing that will give us the following equations for Present Value (PV):

From the equation:

$$FV = PV\left(1 + \frac{r}{m}\right)^{mn}$$

We have,

$$PV = \frac{FV}{(1 + \frac{r}{m})^{mn}}$$

If the conversion period is once a year (m=1), then the formula reduces to:

$$PV = \frac{FV}{(1 + r)^n}$$

This is the formula for the Present Value (PV) for a future sum FV, discounted at r% interest for n years.

Example 4: *What is the Present Value of an investment that will result in a future sum of $100,000 within a period of 5 years @ a discount rate of 10% per annum, converted annually?*

Here FV=100,000; r=10% (0.1) and n=5. Substituting these values in the equation above, gives the following:

$$PV = \frac{100,00}{(1 + 0.1)^5} = \frac{100,000}{(1.61)} = 62,111.80$$

Thus, the future amount, $100,000, expected in five years' time, is worth about $62,000 only today, based on the discounting rate of 10% per annum.

Below is a table from, **ExpressBook iPMA** accounting software for real estate, showing the Present Values Schedule for an investment worth $500,000 in 5 years, discounted at a 10% discount rate:

PRESENT VALUES SCHEDULE					
Year	Date	Interest Factor		PV	Currency
5	01/08/2025	0.62		310,450.00	US Dollar
4	01/08/2024	0.68		341,500.00	US Dollar
3	01/08/2023	0.75		375,650.00	US Dollar
2	01/08/2022	0.83		413,200.00	US Dollar
1	01/08/2021	0.91		454,550.00	US Dollar
0	01/08/2020	1.00		500,000.00	US Dollar

Note: The table displays the Present Value (PV) for each year, along with the Discount Factor, from bottom to top. The final figure (Year 5) is the amount the Investment is worth if one were to pay for it now, and that amount is $310,450.

Present Value of An Annuity

Future Value Annuity (FVA) involves accumulated series of payments to obtain a future sum. Present Value Annuity (PVA), on the other hand, involves an individual investing a fixed discounted amount today, in exchange for a fixed monthly or yearly receipt, over a period. Instead of receiving a lump sum at the end of the investment, the individual who makes the investment receives periodic payments for several years to liquidate the investment. Think of it as you are giving somebody a loan and the person paying back the loan through monthly instalments, until the loan is fully paid.

In the previous example, we were dealing with a one-time receipt of an amount equivalent to a future sum. Now, we are going to treat the case where the receipts or payments (depending on whether you are the client or the investor) to liquidate the future sum are made in instalments. Here again, we will work have to work backward using the formula for Future Value of an annuity.

From the Future Value equation,

$$FV = PV(1 + r)^n$$

If we make PV the subject, we have,

$$PV = FV \left[\frac{1}{(1 + r)^n} \right]$$

To obtain a formula for Present Value Annuity (PVA), we replace FV in above formula with R, representing series of receipts, and expand the series over n years:

$$PVA = R\left[\frac{1}{(1+r)^1} + \frac{1}{(1+r)^2} + \frac{1}{(1+r)^3} + \dots + \frac{1}{(1+r)^n}\right]$$

This can be compressed to:

$$PVA = R\sum_{t=1}^{n}\left[\frac{1}{(1+r)^t}\right]$$

This is the equation for computing the Present Value of a future sum, resulting from a yearly receipt **R**, over **n** years, based on a discounting rate of **r**% per annum. However, if the discounting rate is stated per month and the conversion period is **m** times a year, then the general form of this equation is:

$$PVA = R\sum_{t=1}^{mn}\left[\frac{1}{(1+\frac{r}{12})^t}\right]$$

When the bank gives you a loan and asks you to pay a fixed amount every month for a given time to liquidate the loan, this is the formula used for the computation. Real Estate also uses this formula to compute monthly or yearly payments for mortgage or finance leases. If you were to make a full one-time payment for the property, you would have paid PVA, but by making small recurrent payments over many years, you end up paying more, because of the time-value of money, represented by the discounting (or interest) rate. Technically, it is assumed that the person you are making this payment to has already paid for this property at its present value, and you are making these payments to acquire it in the future.

Example 5a: A client needs an investment that can guarantee a steady income of $2,500 every year for 4 years, and her investor insists on 10% annual return, discounted annually. How much should the investor collect from this client today?

$$PVA = R\left[\frac{1}{(1+r)^1} + \frac{1}{(1+r)^2} + \frac{1}{(1+r)^3} \dots + \frac{1}{(1+r)^n}\right]$$

$$PVA = \$2,500\left[\frac{1}{(1+0.1)^1} + \frac{1}{(1+0.1)^2} + \frac{1}{(1+0.1)^3} + \frac{1}{(1+0.1)^4}\right] = \$7,924.66$$

In this second example, you are the investor.

Example 5b: There is an investment that guarantees a yearly cash flow $25,000 for 5 years. Given a discount rate of 10% per annum, how much will you pay today to acquire that portfolio?

Below is the answer to the question, based on the result generated from **ExpressBook iPMA**. From the table, the final figure (Year 1) is the amount this investment is worth today, and that amount is $94,767.50.

	Year	Date	Annuity	Interest Factor	PV	Currency
			PRESENT VALUE ANNUITY SCHEDULE			
	5	01/08/2025	25,000.00	0.62	15,522.50	US Dollar
	4	01/08/2024	25,000.00	1.30	32,597.50	US Dollar
	3	01/08/2023	25,000.00	2.06	51,380.00	US Dollar
	2	01/08/2022	25,000.00	2.88	72,040.00	US Dollar
▶	1	01/08/2021	25,000.00	3.79	94,767.50	US Dollar

Sinking Fund

So far, we have considered the following cases involving annuity (series of recursive payments and receipts) over an interval at a given interest (or discount) rate. The series of payments or receipts were known and fixed. The question we want to answer now is determining the amount required to accumulate to a certain sum on a future date at a given interest rate. Examples include determining the series of monthly or yearly payments required to liquidate a debt; and determining how much to set aside monthly or yearly to acquire an asset. In each of these cases, the future value is known, the interest rate is known, and the duration (number of years) required to accumulate to the future value is known. What is not known is the series of payments necessary to arrive at the future value.

The solution to this problem is encapsulated in the Future Value of Annuity (FVA) formula:

$$FVA = P \sum_{t=1}^{n.-1} (1 + r)^t + P$$

We need to make P, the recursive payments, the subject of this formula:

$$P = FVA \sum_{t=1}^{n-1} \left[\frac{1}{(1 + r)^t + 1} \right]$$

This is the formula for finding the yearly recurrent payment (P) that will accumulate to a future sum (FVA) in n years at an annual interest rate i.

The expression inside the braces,

$$\left[\frac{1}{(1 + r)^t + 1}\right]$$

Is called **Sinking Fund Factor (SSF)** in Real Estate, and this accumulation of recurrent payment to a future sum is also referred to as **Sinking Fund**.

If the recurrent payment is monthly, with a monthly conversion period, this formula becomes:

$$P = FVA \sum_{t=1}^{12n-1} \left[\frac{1}{\left(1 + \frac{r}{12}\right)^t + 1}\right]$$

Example 6: How much yearly savings will be required to accumulate to **$25,000** in **5 years** at an annual interest rate of **10%**, compounded yearly over a period of 5 years?

$$P = \$25,000 \sum_{t=1}^{4} \left[\frac{1}{(1 + 0.1)^t + 1}\right] = 25,000 \left[\frac{1}{6.11}\right] = \$4,091.65$$

The issue of rounding error will always affect the result from manual calculations. The value obtained for this same problem from **ExpressBook iPMA** is $4,094.94. The result obtained from the software by using this annuity value to compute Future Value Annuity (FVA) is as shown on the Table below:

	Period	Date	Annuity	Interest Factor	FV
FUTURE VALUE ANNUITY RECEIPTS OR PAYMENTS SCHEDULE					
▶	1	30/07/2020	4,094.94	1.00	4,094.94
	2	30/07/2021	4,094.94	2.10	8,599.37
	3	30/07/2022	4,094.94	3.31	13,554.25
	4	30/07/2023	4,094.94	4.64	19,004.62
	5	30/07/2024	4,094.94	6.11	25,000.02

INTERNAL RATE OF RETURN (IRR)

The four primary variables involved in all the formula we have discussed so far are as follows:

a) **FV(A)** = Future Value
b) **PV(A)** = Present Value
c) **r** = rate (interest or discount)
d) **n** = time

Out of these four, three will always be known, and our task always involved finding the value of the unknown. So far, we have solved the problem for the first two of these variables. What is referred to as Internal Rate of Return is nothing other than finding **r** when all the other variables are known.

Thus, the **Internal Rate of Return (IRR)**—also referred to as *Yield*— answers the question: *If both the Present and Future Value of an investment is known, what is the interest rate it will yield over a period of n years?*

We will answer this question for two types of investments, namely:

a) Investment with a single receipt
b) Investment with periodic recurrent receipts (Investment Annuity)

IRR For a Single Receipt Investment

From the Present Value equation, we have to make r the subject of the formula:

$$PV = FV \left[\frac{1}{(1+r)^n} \right]$$

$$PV(1+r)^n = FV$$

$$(1+r)^n = \frac{FV}{PV}$$

$$(1+r) = \left(\frac{FV}{PV} \right)^{1/n}$$

Finally,

$$r = \left[\left(\frac{FV}{PV} \right)^{1/n} - 1 \right]$$

Example 7: A property is available for sale now at **$250,000**. This property is expected to appreciate to a value of **$650,000** after **10 years**. Find the rate of interest (or yield) an investor can earn if he buys this property and holds it for 10 years.

From the formula above:

$$r = \left[\left(\frac{650,000}{250,000}\right)^{1/10} - 1\right] = [(2.6)^{0.1} - 1] = 0.1 = \mathbf{10\%}$$

This will allow the investor to compare this result with IRR other investment options before the final decision to invest.

The IRR schedule for each of the 10 years, obtained from **ExpressBook iPMA**, is as shown below:

	Year	Date	PV	FV	IRR (%)
			IRR SCHEDULE		
	1	01/08/2021	250,000.00	650,000.00	160.00
	2	01/08/2022	250,000.00	650,000.00	61.25
	3	01/08/2023	250,000.00	650,000.00	37.51
	4	01/08/2024	250,000.00	650,000.00	26.98
	5	01/08/2025	250,000.00	650,000.00	21.06
	6	01/08/2026	250,000.00	650,000.00	17.26
	7	01/08/2027	250,000.00	650,000.00	14.63
	8	01/08/2028	250,000.00	650,000.00	12.69
	9	01/08/2029	250,000.00	650,000.00	11.20
▶	10	01/08/2030	250,000.00	650,000.00	10.03

We are only interested in the 10th year IRR figure, which is approximately 10%.